A Girl

and

Her Dogs

Carol Norris
and
Kelsey Anastasia Norris

ISBN 978-1-64299-380-6 (paperback)
ISBN 978-1-64299-381-3 (digital)

Christian Faith Publishing, Inc.
832 Park Avenue
Meadville, PA 16335
www.christianfaithpublishing.com

Cover photo credit: Tamara Joiner

Printed in the United States of America

Every Hero Has a Story

This is a story about a girl and her dogs. The girl is my daughter Kelsey and the dogs are named Sadie and Izzie. The four of us are a family united by love and separated through the cruelty of other humans. The only way Kelsey and I can deal with our tragic loss is to write about it. That is why you are reading this book today.

I found Kelsey, in a Russian orphanage, when she was eleven months old and weighing less than fourteen pounds. Alone, sick, starving, and emaciated, her head had been shaved due to lice. She was dressed in rags and had never worn a diaper. The doctors did not know if she would ever walk or talk. Despite these issues, she had big bright eyes, lots of energy, and her enthusiasm for life captured everyone's attention. I fell in love with her the minute I met her and decided to adopt her as a single parent.

Kelsey at the orphanage in November 2004.

Kelsey is currently a fourteen-year-old seventh grade autistic special education student in the local public middle school. Diagnosed as having intellectual disabilities and Rubinstein-Taybi Syndrome (a rare genetic disorder), she has been educated in a self-contained special education classroom since she was in the second grade. She is thriving and is on the honor roll, and is a member of the National Junior Beta Club. This success did not happen overnight. During the past twelve years, I have worked tirelessly to make certain that she received the medical care, speech/physical therapy, nutrition, and other supportive resources she needs to be successful. There are so many wonderful friends, doctors, therapists, teachers, and coaches that have supported and helped develop her during the past twelve years.

Kelsey is not your typical seventh grade student. Currently, Kelsey is a nationally recognized fourteen year old advocate, community volunteer, beauty queen, author, and athlete. By the time she was in seventh grade, Kelsey has provided over 2,500 volunteer hours and raised more than $30,000 for a wide variety of causes aiding children and others in difficult situations. She has received a Hometown Hero award from the American Red Cross, two Kohl's Kids Care Scholarship Program awards, and a National Youth Activist award. She has been named one of the top ten youth volunteers in the nation by the Prudential Spirit of Community award and has received several Presidential Community Service awards signed by the President of the United States. Kelsey has also been honored with official resolutions from her local County Commissioners, Georgia Governor Nathan Deal, the Georgia State Senate, and the Georgia House of Representatives commending her for her work to support Georgia children who are in crisis and in other difficult circumstances.

None of this success would have been possible if not for the love of her two dogs, Sadie and Izzie. When Kelsey was in first grade, she was tiny and only weighed approximately forty pounds. She was struggling to survive in school. She was the victim of merciless bullying and emotional abuse. Much of this was led by her classroom teacher who did not know how to appropriately interact with special needs children. She even told Kelsey that she was dumb and a bad girl. Kelsey was not the only student bullied in the classroom that year, but she was the one that I was responsible for protecting. It was heartbreaking to see her come home every afternoon from school with physical and emotional bruises. As her mother, of course I complained repeatedly and asked (and even begged) for the situation to be resolved appropriately, including requesting that she be moved to another classroom. Nothing seemed to help until the school became concerned that I and some of the other parents might seek legal action against them. Eventually, Kelsey stuck it out and was promoted to the next grade.

One of the happiest days that I have experienced as a parent was on her last day of school in first grade. Kelsey and I walked out of the school knowing that she would never again be left alone in that classroom. It took Kelsey several years to overcome the damage that had been inflicted that year. She was still scared to physically enter the school building at the beginning of second grade. Thankfully, starting in second grade, she had wonderful teachers who were trained to teach students using individualized instruction. We are grateful for those special education teachers who not only taught Kelsey how to read and write, but also taught her that school can be a kind and supportive place that values human dignity and the potential that exists for every child, no matter their disability.

However, the most significant turning point in Kelsey's life was the day she met her dog Izzie. Since second grade, Izzie has been her protector, best friend, and confidant. They were joined a few years later by an abandoned puppy named Sadie. It has been the power of this bond, cemented by mutual love, that has forever changed Kelsey's life.

Kelsey Meets Izzie

Kelsey has always loved animals. I remember, on my first visit to the Russian orphanage when I met Kelsey, there were a few worn posters on the wall in the room where Kelsey and the other orphans were housed. All of the workers only spoke Russian and I needed to bring a translator with me in order to communicate with them. One of the workers said she wanted to show me something. She looked at Kelsey and said "cat" in Russian and Kelsey immediately smiled and clapped her hands and pointed to the poster. At that point, she had never seen a real cat, but she had decided she liked them.

During my first several hours with Kelsey at the orphanage, I held her tightly and sang to her in English. She looked at me like I was some type of foreign space alien who was speaking in a strange language. The song she liked that I was singing over and over again was "Mary had a little lamb." She smiled every time I started to sing the song again.

Kelsey with her first stuffed animal, Rosie the lamb.

Once we arrived home in Georgia, we immediately started her stuffed animal collection. Our house soon became full of all types of stuffed animals. She preferred the stuffed animals over her dolls. Her first favorite stuffed animal was a little pink lamb she named Rosie. During her first couple of years at home, she carried Rosie everywhere she went.

As much as she loved her stuffed animals, she loved real ones even more. Every time she saw a puppy or a cat, she wanted to pet and hold them. By the time she was four, she was begging me just about every day to buy her a puppy. I wanted to wait until she was older and could start taking care of a pet before we introduced one into our household. That strategy worked until she started experiencing the heartbreaking bullying episodes during first grade. Every night she came home from school with bruises, crying and feeling like she did not have a friend in the world. It helped that she was very busy after school in a variety of extracurricular community activities including cheerleading, gymnastics, and dance. During those community based activities, she interacted with many children and had many friends she looked forward to interacting with each week. However, something was still missing in her life.

When she turned eight, I decided it was time to begin looking for a dog. I did not want to buy one from a store. I wanted to find just the right rescue dog that needed a good home. One of my friends, Debbie Connell, sent me a picture of a rescue dog named Izzie that was looking for a loving home. Izzie was approximately seven months old and was being fostered by a family of dog lovers. Apparently, a Good Samaritan almost ran over Izzie when she was approximately six weeks old on an isolated rural Georgia road. Someone had dumped her along the side of the road and left her to die. He stopped and put Izzie in his car and drove her to the family's house that he knew would take care of her. Several months later, that family realized it was time for Izzie to find her forever home and distributed her picture, encouraging someone to adopt her.

Kelsey meeting Izzie in December 2011.

When I saw Izzie's picture, I told Debbie that I was very interested and wanted to meet Izzie. After meeting Izzie a few days later, I decided that she would be perfect for our family. The next Saturday, when Kelsey was home from school, I took Kelsey to meet Izzie and bring her home. I think it was the happiest day of Kelsey's life.

Kelsey bringing Izzie home in December 2011.

At that time she was still not very verbal. She had been working with speech therapists for several years. They had made progress, but Kelsey still wasn't spending much time speaking in complete sentences to other people. When she met Izzie for the first time, her face lit up like a Christmas tree. She hugged her and would not let go of her the entire forty-five-minute drive home.

When we arrived home, Kelsey showed Izzie every room in the entire house and then took her outside in the backyard to play. The backyard became their kingdom. We have a big backyard (approximately one acre) that has a six feet wooden privacy/security fence surrounding it. There are plenty of trees, a swing set, an enclosed pool, and a big enclosed trampoline. The two of them spent hours every day after school and on weekends exploring the backyard and playing imaginary games. Kelsey decided that Izzie was her BFF (best friend forever). Their most favorite place to play in the backyard was Kelsey's trampoline. Kelsey loved jumping on it and Izzie soon learned to jump with her. I became so accustomed to seeing them jump together that it seemed very natural to me. Other adults, however, who saw them jumping together for the first time always were shocked to see a dog jumping on her hind legs like a human with a smile on her face.

The most amazing thing about their friendship, however, was the immediate change in Kelsey. She would spend hours sitting on the trampoline with Izzie, reading to her. Kelsey took her story books outside to the trampoline every afternoon, and they would read together until it was too dark to see the pages. Kelsey would also talk to Izzie in complete sentences, telling her about her day at school and talking about what she wanted to do when she grew up.

Kelsey playing in the backyard with Izzie.

One of the most touching things that Kelsey and Izzie did each evening was to pray together. Kelsey spent hours teaching Izzie the prayers and bible verses that she was learning in Sunday school. Kelsey would repeat them over and over again to Izzie until Kelsey had memorized them. Then every evening, Kelsey would pray with Izzie, and while Kelsey was reciting the Lord's Prayer, Izzie would bow her head. It seemed as if Izzie was also praying. I cried every time I watched them together. Izzie quickly became an integral part of our family.

Missing

The most frightening day of my life occurred on Friday, January 27, 2012. Kelsey loved to play with Izzie when she came home from school (especially on Friday nights, because she did not have any of her extracurricular activities after school). I keep all of our doors locked with the exception of the back door when Kelsey is in the backyard playing. There are three gates to the backyard that are always kept padlocked. When the pool or yard people need to get into the backyard, they have to knock on the front door and ask me to unlock one of the gates. I am the only person who has keys to the backyard gates.

On that Friday afternoon, Kelsey and Izzie were playing in the backyard, and I went into the house to answer the phone. Kelsey's teacher was calling me with good news about a test Kelsey took at school earlier that day. We talked for fifteen to twenty minutes, and I went back outside to feed Izzie. When I walked outside the back door, I could not find Kelsey and Izzie. They were not in the backyard. Since I thought that there was no other way to get out of the backyard other than to come into the house, I immediately assumed that somehow I had not seen them when they decided to come back into the house. I searched the first floor of the house and could not find them. I then assumed that they must be upstairs playing in Kelsey's room. When I checked, there was no one upstairs. I immediately methodically searched every room in the house, including all closets and the garage. They were not in the house. Then I looked through the back window and saw the pool. I immediately panicked because, in my mind, that was the only other place they could be. By that time, it was starting to get dark, and I had to turn on the pool lights to look into the pool. Thank goodness, they were not there.

By that time, I had run out of options regarding where to look. They had vanished. I could not figure out how they had be able to leave the backyard. Even though I knew that it was highly unlikely that they were in the front yard or anywhere else in the neighborhood, I ran around the front yard and down the street calling their names. No one helped me or expressed any concern regarding a missing child. At that point, I called 911 and told them that there was a special needs child and her dog that were missing. After getting a description of Kelsey and Izzie, the 911 operator told me to stay at home and wait for the sheriff's deputies. I also called Kelsey's godparents, Nancy and Mike. Mike was the police chief in Butler, Georgia and it is about a one hour drive. Nancy told me that they were on their way to help. Afterward, Nancy told me that within five minutes of my call, Mike had his car loaded with his guns, search gear, big flashlights, and some type of search spotlights.

While I was waiting for everyone to arrive, I kept running around the backyard and the front of the house calling Kelsey's name. Just after the sun went down, I thought I heard a child crying and a dog barking. At first it was very faint, and then it started to get louder, and it seemed like it was coming from the back of the house. I ran into the backyard screaming Kelsey's name. It was very dark and I could only see a few yards in front of me. Just then, Izzie ran towards me with Kelsey running behind her, crying for me. They both were soaked from head to toe and they were covered in mud. They both were very upset.

After questioning Kelsey, we determined that Izzie had dug a hole under the fence at the back of our property and climbed under it. Kelsey was worried about Izzie and followed her under the fence. Kelsey said that, at some point, she fell into a "swamp" and was lying in the water and could not get up. Izzie, apparently, kept trying to grab the fabric of her pink Disney princess sweatshirt with her teeth. The scratch and teeth marks on Kelsey's right shoulder supported Kelsey's story. Izzie was pulling on the fabric around the shoulder and hood of her sweatshirt to get Kelsey to stand up and get out of the water. Kelsey said she could not find her way home because all she saw were fences, (Many of my neighbors have the same type of six foot fence that we have). Kelsey said that she followed Izzie, and Izzie stopped at one of the fences and started to dig under the fence. She followed Izzie under the fence, and it was into our backyard.

The most frightening aspect of this scenario is that the landscape changes a few feet from our back property line. There is some type of a drop off into a gully with running water (after it rains). Kelsey must have fallen into the gully. There are no houses behind us because we adjoin the 12,750 acre Oaky Woods Wildlife Management Area. It is supposed to have bobcats, foxes, coyotes, black bears, wild hogs, snakes, and small game animals. If Izzie had not found her way back to our yard, they would probably have been in the habitat at least for the night. I do not think that the search parties would have been able to do much in the dark in that terrain. If not for Izzie's protective instincts, Kelsey probably would have died that night.

Kelsey was pretty shaken up and was freezing when I found her. I declined an ambulance for her because she seemed okay and would have become more upset if she had to leave home to go to the hospital. After a hot bath (for both her and Izzie) she calmed down and talked to us. Nancy and Mike stayed awhile to talk to her and make certain she was all right. Mike walked the perimeter of our fence with a flashlight and found the place on the fence line where they came back into the yard. He said he could see the claw marks that Kelsey made with her hands and shoes as she was frantically digging through the dirt and mud to follow Izzie back into the yard. He told me to get an invisible fence for Izzie that will not allow her to get close enough to the big fence to dig. The next day, I contacted our lawn service company to fill in the holes under the fence so Kelsey couldn't get out again. I also made arrangements to have an invisible fence installed.

Kelsey had some scratches on her legs and hands but she was okay. She went to her cheerleading game on Saturday and Sunday school on Sunday. Kelsey seemed fine, but it took me several days to calm down. We almost lost her that Friday evening. It should be noted that, according to the National Autism Association, 42% of autism-wandering cases involving a child nine or younger have ended in death and accidental drowning accounts for approximately 90% of lethal outcomes.

Sadie

Our family seemed fairly complete except we began to worry that Izzie might be lonely. As Kelsey grew older, she spent more time at dance performances, practices, pageants, and working on community service projects. She no longer had several hours each afternoon to play with Izzie. We decided that we needed to find a friend for Izzie and started looking for a rescue puppy that would fit into our family.

Kelsey bringing Sadie home.

Right before Christmas, one of our friends posted a picture on Facebook asking if anyone was looking for a puppy. We went to meet the puppies that her sister was fostering. There were several puppies in the litter. Their mother had been a stray who was shot by someone who left the puppies to die. A rescue group found them, and they were being cared for by a foster family. There was one female in the litter who had already been named Sadie. She was feisty and friendly. She was the smallest puppy in the litter and fought her brothers for a place at the food bowl.

Kelsey and Sadie buying a sweater.

Kelsey immediately fell in love with her and wanted to bring her home. Sadie was barely six weeks old, and Kelsey was scared to put her down on the floor. I will never forget when the two dogs met each other on our kitchen floor. Izzie came running into the room when we arrived home that night with Sadie. She did not know what to think. She will never have puppies of her own (she had the operation before we adopted her) and I worried that she would not know how to act around a new puppy. Izzie immediately sniffed Sadie and decided that she would become her mother. From that day forward, the two dogs were inseparable. Sadie followed Izzie everywhere. They slept together, ate together, and played together. The only time they ever became irritated with each other was when one of them thought that Kelsey was giving the other dog too much attention. They both wanted to sit on Kelsey's lap or cuddle with her on the coach or play with her on the floor at the same time. The three of them became three BFFs.

Our Family

The four of us became a close-knit family unit. I never worried about Kelsey when she was in the house or backyard because I knew the dogs were not letting her out of their sight. Every time Kelsey came home from school or an activity she would immediately look for her dogs, and the dogs would be waiting for her. They were fiercely protective and loyal to us.

The Norris girls.

These dogs were more than just our friends and family members. They actually protected us. We both felt safe knowing that they were with us. On one occasion, Izzie even got between Kelsey and a huge rattlesnake that was in our backyard. I will never forget Izzie's bloodcurdling screams as she valiantly fought the snake that kept lunging at her and Kelsey. She fought the snake to the death and probably saved Kelsey's life that day.

On another occasion, I heard the dogs barking in the middle of the night and raised the garage door and looked outside with a flashlight. Out of the corner of my eye, I saw what looked like a bear running across our front lawn from our trash cans. It scared me to death, but I think our dogs' barking scared it away. I should note that bear sightings are not that rare in my neighborhood. Home security cameras have caught pictures of bears rummaging through trash cans in our neighborhood. Remember, we are adjacent to the Oaky Woods Wildlife Management Area, and that habitat continues to get smaller as new subdivisions are being built in the area.

Within the last couple of months, our neighborhood has had numerous home burglaries and automobiles vandalized. A few weeks ago, I had fallen asleep in the den and was awakened by strange noises after midnight. I could hear several male voices talking to each other, and it sounded as if they were trying to manually lift our garage door. I was frightened and peered out the side window to try to see what was going on. The dogs immediately started barking ferociously, and the strangers ran away down the driveway.

The three best friends watching TV.

I believe our dogs would have done anything they could to protect us. Neither of them had any type of special training, but they seemed to instinctively know what we needed. I am a diabetic, and on occasion, my blood sugar will get dangerously low. One night, Sadie woke me up by barking and licking my face. She had sensed that something was wrong with me. When I woke, I was shaking, feeling dizzy, and sweating. I realized that my blood sugar was low, and I needed to immediately eat or drink something with sugar in it. I tried to get up and felt the room spinning. I told Sadie that I needed Kelsey's candy. The dogs were always watching Kelsey eat, and they especially liked to eat her treats when she left them laying on the coffee table or on the counter. Sadie left the room and returned a few minutes later with a half-eaten bag of gummi bears for me to eat. After eating a few of them, I was able to raise my blood sugar level and feel better.

These are just a few examples of how our dogs loved and cared for us. We felt happier and safer when they were with us. We thought we would spend at least the next ten years with our fur babies. I dreaded the day that they would become old and die. I thought that would be unbearable.

The Saddest Day of Our Lives

Wednesday, October 3, 2017, started out as a typical school day. My alarm went off at five thirty in the morning so I could wake Kelsey up at five forty-five to get ready for school. As she did every morning, the first thing Kelsey did was take the dogs outside into the backyard and feed them. As I had to do every morning, I called her in from the backyard and told her she had to say goodbye to the dogs because it was time to eat breakfast and get ready for school. She gave the dogs their daily morning hug and told them that she would tell them all about her school day when she returned home that afternoon. When the school bus picked her up at six fifty, she was happy and eager to start her school day.

Kelsey is an animal rights advocate.
Photo credit: Bonnie Rebholz

The dogs played in the backyard that morning enjoying chasing squirrels and rabbits. Everything seemed so very normal and serene. At nine in the morning, I was in the shower getting ready for work when I thought I heard a loud banging on my front door. I turned off the water and heard another loud banging noise. It startled me and I slipped getting out of the shower and fell (the strength and balance in my legs were not yet fully recovered from a recent hospital stay in the critical care unit and subsequent outpatient dialysis treatments). I almost panicked and was scared that there was some sort of emergency at my front door. I struggled, trying to ignore the pain, to pull myself up off the floor and throw on some clothes. I rely on a walker to be able to walk and I slowly moved as fast as possible given the circumstances. By the time I was able to get to the front door, I encountered two angry animal control officers from the county. They had two large official county vehicles with flashing lights in front of my house. I must admit I was scared to death to see this spectacle in my front yard.

One of the officers asked me if I was the owner of two dogs. I said yes, and he proceeded to tell me that they had a complaint that there were two large vicious dogs roaming the neighborhood scaring families who were afraid to leave their homes. I was speechless and in a state of shock to think that he was referring to Sadie and Izzie. Just then, I heard them barking at my neighbor's dogs on the side of my house. I told the officers to wait a minute, and I went to my side garage door. I opened the garage door and found Sadie and Izzie in our driveway barking at the neighbor's dogs (who were behind a wrought iron fence in their yard). The neighbor's dogs were also agitated and barking at my dogs. I yelled, "Sadie and Izzie." When they heard their names, they ran like lightning bolts into our garage and into the house with me.

I returned to the front door and informed the officers that the dogs were now in the house, and I did not know how they had gotten out of the backyard. One of the officers told me that one of my neighbors had videoed the dogs jumping over our fence, and they had acted viciously to him. He proceeded to inform me that this was not the first time this had happened, and the neighbor had complained to them on previous occasions. I listened and let the words sink in. Then I asked him why no one had ever called me about this. They said that no one had my telephone number, and they had no way of contacting me. I told them that this was obviously not true. My neighbors had my telephone number, and the county even had my number. I am on their emergency alert system and the county is constantly notifying me of any impending storm and emergency situations.

I also told him that they had just seen how easy it was for me to call the dogs back into the house. When my dogs had gotten out on previous occasions, they had become upset when they could not figure out how to get back in to the backyard. Usually, they dug holes under the fence to get out and explore. I have previously spent thousands of dollars on paying someone to install an invisible fence (three times) which the dogs subsequently figured a way out of by chewing the wires and chewing off each other's security collars. I also spent thousands of dollars on paying my lawn service company to put bricks, chicken wire, and even concrete at the base of my fence to cover all holes and other places they are likely to dig. During the last five years, we have responsibly taken every possible step to keep our dogs secure and safe in our backyard.

The other interesting fact is that I understand that Izzie can jump. In fact, one of her favorite pastimes is jumping on the trampoline with Kelsey. Sadie, on the other hand, is smaller and doesn't jump. She is even scared to go upstairs, so we have to carry her up and down the stairs. I can't imagine her easily jumping over a six foot fence. No one has shown me the video that allegedly exists showing them both jumping over the fence. Furthermore, our backyard fence has three heavy-duty security locks that stay locked almost all of the time (including the morning of the incident). It is true, when I called them in the house they somehow had managed to get out into the driveway. It would have been helpful if someone could have adequately explained how they got there.

The other peculiar fact about this sudden concern about "vicious" dogs roaming the neighborhood is that dogs accidentally get out of yards in our neighborhood on a frequent basis. The neighborhood association's Facebook page is full of posts with pictures of over seventy-five dogs that have been found in other people's yards during the past year. In fact, a few days before, we had found a strange dog in our driveway who was barking at our dogs in the backyard who were subsequently barking back at him. Instead of calling 911 to report a "vicious" dog in the neighborhood, I posted his picture on the neighborhood association's Facebook page asking if anyone knew who this dog belonged to. This is what good neighbors do for each other.

I was shaking with anger to think that anyone in my neighborhood would sit and wait until my dogs supposedly jumped the fence so they could videotape them and subsequently call 911 to tell them that "vicious" dogs were roaming the neighborhood without a leash. I apologized for my dogs getting out of the backyard, and told the officers that I would try to make certain that they did not do it again. They said that was not good enough. He gave me two citations for not restraining my animals (leash law violation) and a notice to appear in court later that month. They also informed me to not let the dogs out of the house until this situation was resolved. I attempted to explain to the officers that this was part of a bigger issue that was not about the dogs, and they did not want to hear about it. It is ironic because I am fairly confident that few, if any, of the owners of the other seventy-five dogs that were found roaming unleashed in my neighborhood were given a citation, court appearance order, and a several hundred dollar fine. It is significant that the family of a small autistic child with intellectual disabilities is the one family who was singled out to suffer negative consequences when the other incidents were ignored.

After the officers left, I went back into the house and locked the door. A couple of days prior to this incident, we had received an anonymous note left in our mailbox. The poorly worded message warned us that we needed to be careful because anything could happen to our dogs. The ominous warning implied that our dogs were not safe. I must admit that we have many wonderful neighbors but I was aware that one or more of my neighbors did not like the fact that a family with a special needs child is living in the neighborhood.

Apparently, they feel that they do not want to see a special needs child with intellectual disabilities happily playing with her dogs in the front yard when they drive by our house. In their minds, this scene is bad for home property values.

I began to shake in fear for my child and her dogs. I realized during the encounter with the officers that whoever was targeting my child and her dogs was not going to stop. This was an orchestrated attempt to drive us out of the neighborhood, and that was just a matter of time before the dogs would accidentally get out of the yard again. I was afraid that they eventually would be either poisoned or shot by these people who seemed so determined to get rid of us. I was even more afraid of my child being hurt in the process. It was my duty to protect them even if it meant our dogs needed to be somewhere safe without us. I cried for over an hour at the injustice of this situation that was treating our beloved pets as collateral damage. However, this had been our home for over thirteen years, and we could not afford to move. I know that our situation is not unique. Discrimination against the developmentally disabled is far too common in our country, and our neighborhood is just another example of this unjust and ugly reality for far too many special needs children and their families.

I called the director of the Flint Humane Society and told her about our situation. Kelsey has been a big supporter of that organization and has collected over 6,000 pounds of dog food donations (over three tons) for them. She also designated them to receive a donation check for $5,000 when she won the National Prudential Spirit of Community award earlier that year. We knew they did great work and cared deeply about animals. After hearing our plight, the director told me to bring Sadie and Izzie to them. She said that they would protect them.

I loaded Izzie and Sadie into the car. They looked at me with trusting eyes knowing that their mommy would protect them. I cried the entire one-and-a-half-hour drive to the Flint Humane Society office. The dogs knew something was wrong and tried to kiss me and lick my face while I was driving. It was the saddest and most emotional drive of my life. All I could think about was how I had let them down and failed to protect them. When we arrived at the Flint Humane Society, I took Sadie and Izzie into the lobby. We had a group of volunteers and board members waiting for us. They sat with me and got to know the two dogs who shook their hands with their paws. I was sobbing uncontrollably and did not stop until a little toddler (who was in the lobby with his mother) went up to the "vicious" dogs and kissed and hugged them. That was God's way of telling me that Sadie and Izzie were going to meet new friends who would love and take care of them. The good people at the Flint Humane Society told me that they were going to keep Izzie and Sadie together and they would go home with them that night. I needed to return home to meet Kelsey when the school bus dropped her off after school, so I quietly said goodbye to our fur babies and left the building. I cried all of the way home realizing that I had never cried like this in my entire life.

The worst part of the day was telling Kelsey that she would probably never see her dogs again. She didn't believe me when I first told her the dogs were not in the backyard. She went into the backyard and called their names. She finally sat on the back porch area next to their food and water bowls and sobbed uncontrollably. She had just lost her best friends and never had the opportunity to say goodbye. It was a rough evening. She didn't want to eat and didn't want to talk about it until after nine in the evening (when she should have already been asleep). Kelsey asked me why people could be so mean and why God would allow this to happen. I told her that I did not know, but I knew that God loved us and he loved Sadie and Izzie. She took comfort in the fact that Sadie and Izzie were with good people who loved them. However, she cried herself to sleep in my arms.

Kelsey mourning the loss of her two best friends
Photo credit: Bonnie Rebholz

In the days since that horrible day, Kelsey has been sad and lonely. She attempts to go about her daily routine of school, extra-curricular activities and community service projects. However, I can sense her quiet despair and sadness. I have contacted our friends at the Flint Humane Society to check on Sadie and Izzie numerous times. They are doing well. At the time we are finishing writing this book, the Flint Humane Society has worked with an organization to ensure that they have been adopted and are currently in good situations.

Our attorney feels we did the right thing by attempting to de-escalate the situation and keep our dogs safe. Since Sadie and Izzie have been gone, our neighborhood is still not safe. Pets have gone missing with some coming home shot. Others have been found dead. I thank God every night that Sadie and Izzie are safe and have not been injured or killed.

Sadie and Izzie will always be part of our family. A piece of our hearts is missing, and we pray for them every night. The only thing they are guilty of is loving and protecting my daughter. Even though it remains a hostile atmosphere, we are not moving from our neighborhood. Life can be unjust and unfair, especially in a neighborhood not known for its diversity or acceptance. However, I am teaching my daughter that you do not run from bullies. Instead, you stand up to them with kindness and resolve. We pray for those people that are willing to deliberately be cruel and torment children with developmental disabilities and their pets. Perhaps, God can help them see the light and become better human beings.

In the meantime, Kelsey will continue to be a strong advocate for no-kill animal shelters. She will continue to support the Flint Humane Society and other shelters that are dedicated to protecting innocent animals. We are all God's creatures and we have a responsibility to protect each other.

Kelsey and Izzie praying together.
Photo credit: Tamara Joiner

About the Author

For more than thirty years, Carol Norris has served as a devoted advocate for nonprofit organizations, public agencies, and community collaboratives that serve children and families. She is the president and senior consultant at Norris Consulting Group. She specializes in grant writing, resource development, strategic planning, and evaluation. Carol has written over three hundred successfully funded grant proposals totaling over $150 million to fund after-school programs, school-based health centers, bullying prevention programs, juvenile delinquency prevention programs, mental health services, child health networks, school wellness programs, and other family support programs. These services have subsequently assisted hundreds of thousands of poor and disadvantaged children and families.

Carol Norris currently resides in Bonaire, Georgia with her fourteen-year-old daughter, Kelsey. She adopted Kelsey, as a single mother, from a Russian orphanage when she was fourteen months old. Kelsey is currently a nationally recognized advocate, community volunteer, beauty queen, author, and athlete. She has been diagnosed as having autism, intellectual disabilities, and Rubinstein-Taybi Syndrome. Kelsey believes that individuals with disabilities can achieve great things in life and make a tremendous difference in the lives of others. When she grows up, she wants to be a role model for others and start her own charitable foundation that will support children with special needs. Carol and Kelsey have coauthored two books and are in the process of writing additional ones.

CPSIA information can be obtained
at www.ICGtesting.com
Printed in the USA
LVHW07s0123210918
590858LV00011B/46/P

9 781642 993806